W9-AJO-566

WITHDRAWN

Rain and the Earth

Nikki Bundey

 Carolrhoda Books, Inc. / Minneapolis

First American edition published in 2001 by
Carolrhoda Books, Inc.

All the words that appear in **bold** type are explained
in the glossary that starts on page 30.

Photographs courtesy of: R. Frans 14 / 16 / Hutchison Picture Library; Norman
Lomax—cover (background) / Impact Photos; Stephen Dalton 10, 22, 23t / Harold
Palo Jr. 12, 26b / Lutra 23b / Eric Soder 24b / NHPA; Kevin Schafer—cover (inset)
left / Martin Harvey—cover (inset) right / Heinrich van den Berg—title page / DERA 4
/ Gordon Wiltsie 5t / David Smiley 6 / S. Krasemann 8 / Alan Watson 15 / Andre
Maslennikov 19 / Nigel J. Dennis 20 / Dylan Garcia 24t / Fritz Polking 25 / Andre
Bartschi 26t / William Campbell 28 / Reinhard Janke 29t / David Drain 29b / Still
Pictures; 17, 21t / The Stock Market; TRIP 5 / J. King 11 / NASA 13 / M. Nichols 18 /
W. Jacobs 21b / Eric Smith 27 / TRIP.

Illustrations by Artistic License/Neil Reed, Genny Haines, Tracy Fennell

Carolrhoda Books, Inc.
A division of Lerner Publishing Group
241 First Avenue North
Minneapolis, Minnesota 55401 U.S.A.

Website: www.lernerbooks.com

All U.S. rights reserved. No part of this book may be reproduced, stored in a retrieval
system, or transmitted, in any form or by any means, electronic, mechanical,
photocopying, recording, or otherwise, without the prior written permission of
Carolrhoda Books, Inc., except for the inclusion of brief quotations in an
acknowledged review.

A ZOË BOOK

Copyright © by 2000 Zoë Books Limited. Originally produced in 2000 by Zoë Books
Limited, Winchester, England

Library of Congress Cataloging-in-Publication Data

Bundey, Nikki, 1948–
   Rain and the earth / by Nikki Bundey
     p. cm. — (The science of weather)
   Includes index.
     Summary: Examines the role that rain plays on earth, how the cycle of
evaporation and condensation works, and the effects of water on all forms of life.
Includes related experiments.
    ISBN 1-57505-469-8 (lib. bdg. : alk. paper)
    1. Rain and rainfall—Juvenile literature. [1. Rain and rainfall. 2. Hydrologic
cycle. 3. Rain and rainfall—Experiments. 4. Experiments. 5. Ecology.] I. Title.
II. Series: Bundey, Nikki, 1948– Science of weather.
QC924.7.B845   2001
551.57'7—dc21   99-40958

Printed in Italy by Grafedit SpA
Bound in the United States of America
1 2 3 4 5 6—OS—06 05 04 03 02 01

CONTENTS

The Rainy Planet	4
It's Raining Again	6
Clouds and Fog	8
Falling Raindrops	10
Splash!	12
Wet Climates	14
Rain for Growing	16
Plants and Water	18
Wildlife and Rain	20
Water Creatures	22
In the Wetlands	24
In the Rain Forests	26
Poison Rain	28
Glossary	30
Index	32

THE RAINY PLANET

Water covers more than two-thirds of the earth. There are great salty oceans, sparkling lakes, and winding rivers. There is even water in the air we breathe. A layer of **gases** surrounds the earth. We call this layer the **atmosphere**. One of the gases is **water vapor**.

From space, astronauts see large areas of the earth covered by blue ocean. Bands of white clouds stream around the planet's atmosphere.

Clouds drop rain onto the earth. Without rain, there would be no life on our planet.

The surface of the planet Mars is a **desert**. Without rain, the earth might look the same. There would be no green grass or blue oceans.

We cannot see water vapor until it turns into a **liquid**. Then, tiny water **droplets** hang in the air as fog or clouds. When the droplets become heavy, they fall to the ground as rain. Rainwater brings life to plants, animals, and people.

5

IT'S RAINING AGAIN

The earth and its atmosphere are like a giant rain factory. Rain making happens over and over again, so we call the process the **water cycle**. The cycle starts when rain falls from the sky onto the planet's surface. The water lies in puddles. It soaks into the ground and drains away into streams, rivers, lakes, and seas.

Mist rises from the ground as the morning sunshine heats water on the earth's surface.

As the sun warms the earth's surface, some water turns into water vapor. This part of the water cycle is called **evaporation**. Hot air rises, carrying the vapor. As the air rises it cools, and the vapor turns into droplets, forming clouds. This process is called **condensation**. Raindrops and snowflakes grow heavy and fall to the earth. This process is called **precipitation**. The water cycle starts over again.

As the droplets grow in size, they fall as drops of rain.

As the air rises, it cools. The water vapor turns into tiny droplets.

Water evaporates from the oceans. Water vapor rises with the warm air.

Rainwater drains into the ground and flows into rivers, lakes, and the ocean.

See for Yourself

Fill two empty yogurt containers with water.
- Cover one container with a lid.
- Leave both containers in a warm place overnight.

- Which container has more water in it the next day? Why?
- Look at the inside of the lid. Which process made the droplets form?

CLOUDS AND FOG

High in the air, water vapor condenses to form clouds. At ground level, condensation causes fog. Clouds form in different shapes and sizes. High in the atmosphere, where the air is very cold, droplets may freeze.

Some clouds can grow to be 600 miles across. Some clouds tower more than 10 miles high and can hold half a million tons of water.

This cloud is called cumulonimbus. It towers high into the sky and may bring a heavy downpour.

Some clouds usually bring rain. If you see cumulonimbus or nimbostratus clouds, reach for your umbrella!

Different types of clouds have different names. Wispy clouds are called *cirrus*. They form about four miles above ground level. Lower down you can see puffy clouds called *cumulus* and blankets of *stratus* clouds. Ten cloud types make up these three main groups.

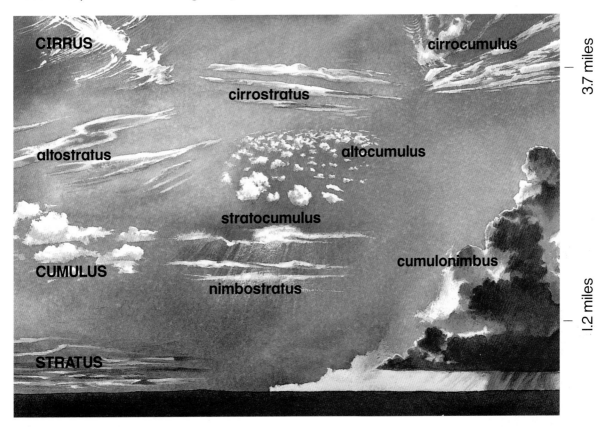

CIRRUS

cirrocumulus

cirrostratus

3.7 miles

altostratus

altocumulus

stratocumulus

cumulonimbus

CUMULUS

nimbostratus

1.2 miles

STRATUS

Cloud type	Mon	Tue	Wed	Thur	Fri	Sat	Sun
Cirrus							
Cirrocumulus							
Cirrostratus							
Altostratus							
Altocumulus							
Stratocumulus							
Cumulonimbus							
Cumulus							
Nimbostratus							
Stratus							

See for Yourself

Make a checklist of all 10 cloud types.
- Over a week, check off those you see.
- Note the **weather** conditions each day.
- Which clouds seem to bring rain?
- Which clouds bring good weather?

FALLING RAINDROPS

Clouds may contain dust and sand, blown into the air by the wind. Wind blows **pollen** from flowering plants, too. The water droplets in clouds gather around these **particles**. When rain falls, the particles fall, too.

Droplets are tiny. It may take a thousand or more to form one drop of rain. Small drops, about one-sixteenth of an inch across, fall in a fine, slow rain called drizzle. In a rainstorm or cloudburst, the drops may be four times bigger.

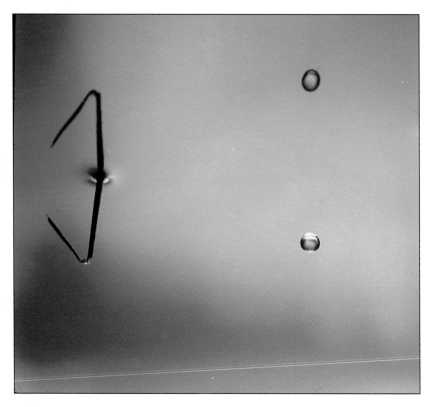

You might expect a raindrop to look like a teardrop, but it is more like a ball. As the drop falls, air presses on it and flattens it.

Strong winds often blow rain sideways as it falls. It falls at an angle, not straight down.

A force called **gravity** pulls rain to the earth. Light drizzle drifts down at a speed of two miles per hour. Big drops in a storm splatter down at about 15 miles per hour. The falling rain can make it hard for people to see clearly.

SPLASH!

Rain may fall into seas or lakes. Rain, rivers, and most lakes are made of **freshwater**, but oceans are salty.

Soft rocks such as limestone soak up rainwater. The water slowly soaks in, until the rocks cannot **absorb** any more. Once the rocks are **saturated**, the water may seep down into underground caves and streams. Rain cannot soak into hard rocks such as granite. When rain cannot drain away, it might flow over the ground, causing a flood.

Rainwater dissolves **minerals** in limestone. As it drips into underground caves, water leaves the minerals behind to form chalky spikes. Spikes that hang from cave roofs are called stalactites. Those that build up from the cave floor are called stalagmites.

This picture of the Ganges River **delta** was taken from space. It shows how rainwater shapes the earth's surface as it drains into the oceans.

Rain can hit the ground hard. Sometimes, the leaves and roots of plants protect the soil. Without plants, the rain may wash the soil away.

Streams and rivers carry along grit and stones. Over many years, the moving water can carve out valleys and canyons. Downstream, sand and mud may wash ashore, forming a beach or mudflat.

See for Yourself

See how water drains through different types of ground.
- Fill four plastic flowerpots with: 1) sand 2) pebbles 3) pebbles with sand on top 4) soil with pebbles on top.
- Place the pots in saucers and leave them out on a rainy night.
- Which pot has the wettest saucer?
- Which pot has the wettest contents?

WET CLIMATES

Sometimes people keep notes about the weather. When it rains a lot in one place over many years, we say that the **climate** there is wet.

Tropical regions, near the **equator**, are warm and wet. Tropical regions have one or two rainy seasons each year. In some parts of India, Central America, and Southeast Asia, more than 70 inches of rain might fall each year

In India, the air gets very hot between March and May. Hot air rises, and ocean winds called **monsoons** rush in to replace the rising air. The winds pick up water from the Indian Ocean and, from June to October, drop heavy rain on the land.

Coastal areas often receive a lot of rain. Mountain ranges may have a rainy side and a dry side. Ocean winds bring rain to the coastal side of the mountain. The opposite side stays dry. The dry region behind the mountains is called a **rain shadow.**

Air currents that blow from the same direction are called **prevailing winds**. In Olympic National Park, in Washington State, prevailing winds blow from the Pacific Ocean. The region has the highest rainfall in the continental United States—about 144 inches each year.

See for Yourself

Do you live in a rainy climate? To find out, measure rainfall in a rain gauge.

- You can make a rain gauge by cutting a plastic bottle in half. Use the top part for a funnel. Use the lower part to collect rain.

- Leave the rain gauge outside on open ground. Every 24 hours, use a ruler to measure the depth of the rainwater. Empty the gauge each day.

- Keep a record of your measurements over several weeks or months.

RAIN FOR GROWING

Rainwater contains a gas called **oxygen**. Plants need water and oxygen to live. Water softens seeds in the soil and helps plants start to grow.

Plant roots absorb water from the ground. They draw it up the stem and into the leaves. Plants use water, a gas called **carbon dioxide**, and sunlight to make food. Water evaporates from the plant through tiny holes. This process is called **transpiration**. A tree may transpire more than 60 gallons of water every day.

A broad leaf has an outer, waterproof layer. Beneath that, you can see the veins that carry water and food around the leaf.

Oaks and maples shed their leaves in autumn. Without leaves, trees can save more water in the winter. Pine needles give out little water, so they stay on the tree.

Plants grow with the seasons. Spring showers and summer sunshine help plants grow and bear fruit. In hot summers, transpiration keeps trees cool. During cold, dark winters, trees must save all the moisture they can.

See for Yourself

How can you prove that plants give out water vapor?

- Cover a house plant with a plastic bag. Fix the open end around the pot with a rubber band.
- Look at your experiment the next day. Have drops of water formed on the inside of the bag?

PLANTS AND WATER

Over thousands of years, plants have **adapted** to rainy and dry conditions. Plants might have long roots to reach moisture deep underground or broad leaves to trap rainwater.

In the desert, rain may fall only once in two or more years. A cactus stores water in its fleshy stem. Some desert seeds can survive for years, waiting for one splash of water that will make them sprout.

The trunk of the baobab tree of tropical Africa is like a barrel. It can store up to 25,000 gallons of water.

See for Yourself

- Line a glass jar with paper towels.

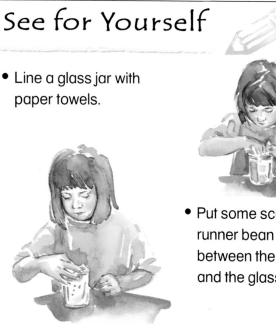

- Put some scarlet runner bean seeds between the paper and the glass.

- Fill the bottom of the jar with water. Add more water as needed to keep the paper damp.

- No matter how you put the bean in, the roots always grow downward.

What invisible force is pulling the roots down?

Duckweed floats on the surface of ponds. The plants have no roots at all. They take in water through their leaves.

Many plants live in damp, boggy ground next to rivers and lakes, where there is always freshwater. Some plants live in the water itself. Most water plants, such as lilies, have roots in rich mud on the lake or river bottom. Other plants float freely.

19

WILDLIFE AND RAIN

Animals absorb water from their food. Some animals feed on plants, others eat animals that eat plants. Animals also take in water directly, by drinking from puddles, ponds, lakes, and rivers.

Water is part of blood, which carries life-giving oxygen through an animal's body. Water helps the animal **digest** food and get rid of waste material. It cools the body down.

Life depends on rain. East Africa's rainy season brings water for wild animals to drink. In dry times, the animals share the few remaining water holes.

When the rainy season arrives, some wild animals **migrate** in search of fresh green pasture.

Slugs and snails need moist **habitats** to survive. Earthworms burrow into damp soil. They come aboveground on rainy nights, when their bodies will not dry out. Long ago, country people believed that worms fell from the sky with the rain.

Some creatures can be a moist habitat themselves. Sloths live in South American forests. During heavy rains, plants called **algae** grow in the sloths' damp fur. They make the fur look green.

Sheep can live in rainy climates. Their wool contains a grease called lanolin. It keeps wool waterproof and shrink-proof.

21

WATER CREATURES

Many animals live in water. There are water **mammals**, such as otters and whales. There are water **reptiles**, such as turtles. Birds such as penguins can swim but not fly.

Mammals and birds need to breathe in oxygen from the air. Fish have developed **gills**, which allow them to take oxygen directly from the water.

This kind of spider lives in ponds. It cannot breathe underwater, so it brings bubbles of air down from the surface.

Frogs lay their spawn in water early in the spring. The jelly contains little black eggs, which hatch when the weather is warmer.

Even a puddle contains tiny life-forms. You can see them if you look at a drop of puddle water through a **microscope**. A pond is full of life, and so is a river or a lake.

Ponds are breeding grounds for all kinds of insects, from dragonflies to mosquitoes. Frogs are **amphibians**. They can live on land or in water. Frogs lay their **spawn** in water. The eggs hatch into tadpoles.

This insect is called a pond skater. It can walk across water. A force called **surface tension** creates a kind of film across the water. The insect can walk on the surface.

IN THE WETLANDS

A rainy climate affects the shape of the land and the lives of plants and animals that live there. It creates a rainy **ecosystem**. The bogs of Ireland are like giant sponges. The average rainfall each year is about 44 inches. The drainage is poor, so water sits in pools. Over thousands of years, plants rot in the water and form a thick layer of soil called **peat**.

Many insects breed in bogs. Some are trapped by sticky, insect-eating plants such as sundew.

A plant called sphagnum moss soaks up large amounts of water. It forms a thick, saturated mat.

Everglades wildlife includes alligators and wading birds such as egrets and spoonbills. There are also deadly snakes such as the water moccasin.

The Everglades are **wetlands** in Florida. The rainfall there averages up to 45 inches each year. Lake Okeechobee drains into the wet, spongy Big Cypress Swamp, and freshwater spills out across 4,000 square miles. The water drains slowly into the sea, through a tangle of saw grass and bear grass, dotted with islands of trees.

IN THE RAIN FORESTS

Up to 150 inches of rain may fall each year on the tropical **rain forests** of Brazil. Water vapor fills the air, making it **humid**. The rain drains into streams and rivers that feed the great Amazon River. The **river basin**, or drainage area, is about 2.7 million square miles.

These warm, wet lands are covered in trees. The treetops form a dense **canopy**, which is home to monkeys and parrots. The canopy shields the forest floor from daylight.

The rain forests of the Amazon are vast. They send a huge amount of water vapor into the atmosphere. People are destroying large areas of rain forest, which is home to millions of plants and animals.

This huge snake is an anaconda. It swims through the water channels of the rain forest. It strangles or drowns its prey.

The Australian island of Tasmania has a temperate climate. Clouds and rainfall sustain forests around Cradle Mountain.

Regions with a cool climate are called **temperate**. Some rainy regions have temperate rain forests—cool, misty forests full of green mosses and ferns. Temperate rain forests are found in eastern Asia, southern Australia (and the island of Tasmania), New Zealand, and North and South America. Olympic National Park in Washington State contains rain forests.

POISON RAIN

Rain affects the land, the oceans, and all living things on earth. During the last 150 years, human activities have poisoned the rainfall.

When we burn fuels such as coal and oil, gases rise into the atmosphere. They mix with water vapor to form acids. Winds may blow the vapor long distances before it falls as **acid rain**. Acid rain damages trees, plants, and even stone buildings.

Acid rain may drain into lakes, killing fish and other creatures. About 4,000 lakes in Sweden are so acidic that fish cannot survive in them.

Rain is a natural cleanser. However, if dangerous chemicals are allowed to pollute land or rivers, rain helps spread the chemicals.

Wildlife and plants live safely in clean, freshwater ponds. Pollution can kill plants and animals. You can help clean up your local environment.

As rainwater drains off the land, it may carry poisons into ditches, streams, and rivers. These poisons include **fertilizers**, weed killers, **pesticides** from farms, and chemical wastes from factories. In many parts of the world, poor drainage and **sewage** systems also poison freshwater.

Poisoning the environment is called **pollution**. We must try not to pollute rainwater. Clean rainwater keeps plants and animals healthy.

GLOSSARY

absorb	Soak up
acid rain	Rain polluted by chemicals in the air
adapted	Changed to survive in particular conditions
algae	A group of simple plants, many of which grow in water
amphibian	An animal such as a frog, living partly on land, partly in water
atmosphere	The layer of gases around a planet
canopy	The upper layer of a forest – the treetops
carbon dioxide	A gas found in the atmosphere, used by plants
climate	The pattern of weather in one place over a long period
condensation	Turning from a gas into a liquid
delta	Land at a river's mouth, shaped by channels of water
desert	An area that receives little or no rainfall
digest	To absorb food into the body
droplet	A tiny drop. Many droplets make up a raindrop
ecosystem	An environment in which animals, plants, and people depend on each other to survive
equator	An imaginary line drawn around the middle of the earth
evaporation	Changing from a liquid into a gas
fertilizers	Chemicals added to soil to help plants grow
freshwater	Salt-free water
gas	An airy substance that fills any space in which it is contained
gills	The organs that allow fish to breathe underwater
gravity	The force that pulls objects to earth
habitat	The normal home of a plant or animal
humid	Containing a high level of water vapor
liquid	A fluid substance, such as water
mammals	Warm-blooded animals that feed their young on milk
microscope	An instrument that enlarges images, helping us to see very tiny objects
migrate	To travel long distances, often to find food
minerals	Substances found in rocks or soil. Gold and silver are minerals

monsoon	A seasonal, rain-bearing wind in southern Asia
oxygen	A life-giving gas found in air and water
particle	A tiny speck or tiny part of a substance
peat	A soil created in a bog by rotting mosses and other plants
pesticides	Chemicals that kill insects on plants or in soil
pollen	Tiny grains that enable flowering plants to reproduce
pollution	Poisoning land, water, or air with chemicals
precipitation	The way in which rain or snow is created in a cloud
prevailing wind	The most common wind direction in a region
rain forest	A forest in a region of high rainfall
rain shadow	A dry region, shielded from rain by high mountains
reptiles	Cold-blooded animals such as snakes and tortoises
river basin	The land from which water drains into a river
saturated	Unable to absorb any more liquid – waterlogged
sewage	Water carrying human waste
spawn	Clumps of eggs in jelly, laid by frogs and toads
surface tension	A force that causes a liquid to act as though it is covered by a thin film
temperate	Having a mild, cool climate
transpiration	The process in which plants give out water vapor
tropical	Describing warm regions to the north and south of the equator
water cycle	The ongoing process in which rain falls, evaporates, rises, and condenses
water vapor	A gas created when water evaporates
weather	Atmospheric conditions such as heat, cold, sun, rain, snow, clouds, and wind
wetland	A moist environment such as a marsh, swamp, or bog

INDEX

air, 4, 5, 7, 8, 15, 22, 26
amphibians, 23
animals, 5, 20, 21, 24
atmosphere, 4, 6, 26

birds, 22, 25, 26
bogs, 24

canopy, 26
carbon dioxide, 16
caves, 12
climate, 14, 15, 21, 24, 27
clouds, 4, 5, 7, 8, 9, 10, 27
condensation, 7, 8

desert, 5, 18
droplets, 5, 7, 8, 10

earth, 4, 5, 6, 7, 22, 28
ecosystem, 24
environment, 29
equator, 14

fish, 22, 28
food, 16, 20
freshwater, 12

gases, 4, 16, 28

habitats, 21

insects, 23, 24

lakes, 4, 6, 12, 19, 20, 23, 25, 28

mammals, 22

mountains, 15, 27

oceans, 4, 5, 12, 13, 14, 15, 28
oxygen, 16, 20, 22

plants, 5, 13, 16, 17, 18, 19, 20, 24, 29
poisons, 28, 29
pollution, 29
ponds, 19, 20, 22, 23, 29

raindrops, 5, 7, 10, 11
rain forests, 26, 27
rainy season, 14, 20, 21
reptiles, 22
rivers, 4, 6, 12, 13, 19, 20, 23, 26, 29
rocks, 12, 13

seasons, 17
seeds, 16, 18, 19
soil, 13, 21, 24
stalactites, 12
stalagmites, 12
storm, 10, 11
swamp, 25

temperate regions, 27
transpiration, 16, 17
tropical regions, 14, 26

waste, 20, 29
water cycle, 6, 7
weather, 9, 14
wetlands, 25
winds, 8, 10, 11, 14, 15, 28